THE GHOST INSIDE ME

Even More Tales from The Baron

BILLY J. BARNUM

First originally published by Billy J. Barnum 2023

ISBN 979-8-218-15179-9 (Paperback)

ISBN 979-8-215-95802-5 (Digital)

Author's signature page

Write me a Poem

She's read thousands of books

But she won't read no more

She said everything out there

Is only a bore

I said there's got to be something

Good to read

She said write me some poetry

And give me what I need

I want claws that dig in

And capture my brain

That make me feel pleasure

That make me feel pain

Like I'm clawing and scratching

Hanging on by a thread

Like my car's flipping over

And I'm losing my leg

Like the monsters from movies

Are coming out of my dreams

As I choke on my spit

When I'm starting to scream

Continued…

Like the words painting pictures

Van Gogh's losing his ear

Like I'm deaf reading lips

Then I'm starting to hear

Make me feel alive

Write those words on the page

Like I'm living in concert

So much dread, so much rage

Then I'll read again

I promise my dear

With your words as my pallet

With the world you will share

Forbidden Box

As I walk into the building

I feel its presence growing near

As I follow the directions

I hear a crowd start to cheer

They keep it locked up in a box

In all its beauty and all its splendor

Holding captive, dangling carrots

As they collect up all the tender

The people disappear

And it's just me, the box, and the attendant

I say "I want to take it out

And hold it in my hands"

He says "I can't let you do that

Or I'll get fired man"

Imprisoned in a box

For the rest of its existence

While gawking eyes they stop to stare

While meeting its resistance

Continued…➡

I want to break in late at night

Lift the box and set it free

Eternity can be its gift

But they'd lock me up and throw away the key

So, I guess that I'll just visit you

Every once in awhile just like everyone else

Like a precious memory in my mind

Categorized and put up on its shelf

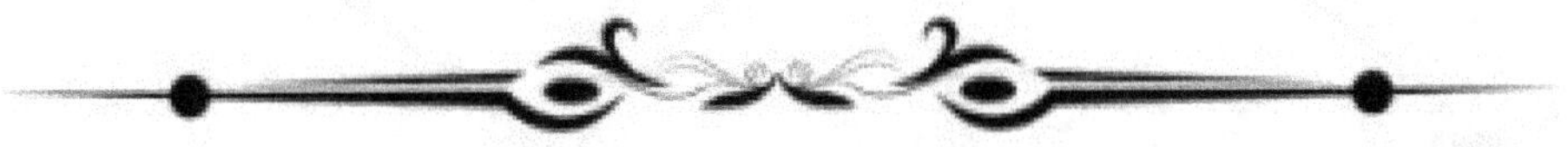

Infatuation

She loved him like a god

Even put him on a pedestal

But she wasn't his cup of tea

Through all the butterflies and windowsills

Staring at the moon

Praying someday he'd be hers

Then the horse went to the stable

Maybe it's time to put away the spurs

He had not a fleeting thought

While she had matrimony in her eyes

He was God, the devil, and everything in between

At night she'd stare at his picture as she softly cried

She'd say to herself "Why don't you see me?"

But her reflection never answered back

As her world was spinning 'round and 'round

She suddenly heard it crack

Then she shattered the mirror

With blood soaking her hand

It was then that she realized

That he would never be her man

HOPE
DESPAIR

Stay on track

Stay on track and believe in yourself

As for all the non-believers they can all just go to hell

It might seem extreme but that's just the way it is

Stay true to your vision and let your imagination live

You've been running so long but not heeding the call

As you see the finish line they build a brick wall

But you've got superpowers and jump right over it

Their words mercilessly beat you as they try to make you quit

But what they don't know is you've got an ace in the hole

And the prayers from the graveyard they are making you grow

And they all stand with angels always having your back

And the only voice that matters keeps saying, just stay on track

A Glorious Host

When you wake in the morning with an ache of the yearn

And the vision of last night, your best friend in an urn

And the feeling of remembrance of the soft silky lips

To the floor as it falls it's the red silky slip

That hugged her so tightly around every curve so sultry

And the night at the restaurant when she ordered the poultry

As you passed her the binoculars to see the stage at the play

It was "The Phantom of the Opera" as they burned all the sage

It may have seemed haunting, a silhouette like a wisp

As her sight was evaded disappearing in the mist

It was all a debauchery entangled leaves on the vine

Like a stopwatch it all stopped with a click on a dime

But the wandering of eyes they see visions so clear

As she's back in her nightgown with her touch growing near

And her whispers so soft, so distinct and atrocious

With the waves as they bellow like the wakes of the ocean

Then she says "I must leave" reads the steam on the mirror

His conscious can't compute must be some type of error

This is the one thing I'll remember the most

She was the Belle of the Ball and a glorious host

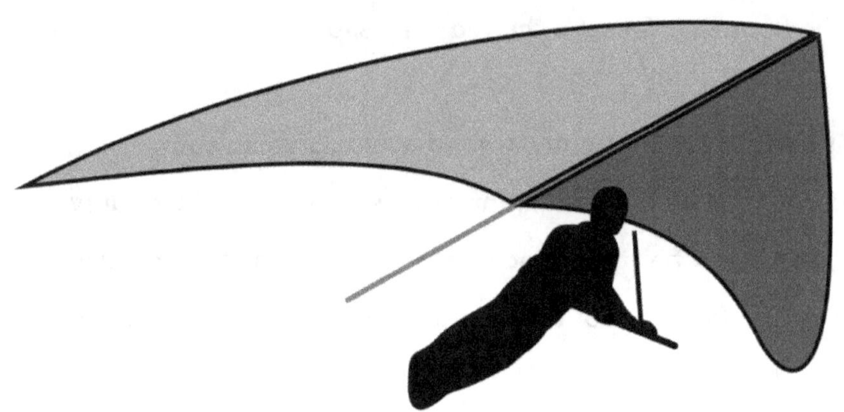

The Hang Glider

He jumped off of the cliff as his eyes grew wider

He was known around town as the unstoppable hang glider

As the winds lift him up and he flies through the clouds

Indescribable freedom as he gets further from the crowds

He had flames on the wings with balls of steel

As the crowds' minds drift trying to imagine how he feels

Hundreds of times he had done this before

With a big run and send off the crowds starting to roar

But this time was different as he starts to descend

The crowds' roars turned to gasps, could this be the end?

The wings snapped and broke off nothing left but the root

As the spectator's cry, he suddenly opens his parachute

They were unaware that he had a backup plan

As they cheered with a song drinking up all their cider

And that's why he was known

As the unstoppable hang glider

The Creepy Castle

The creepy castle on the hill

They walked right by it every day

They'd glance but never stare

While chills ran down their spines in every way

The legend says that there were monsters in that castle

It had a big black steel fence going all around it

And the gate was massive like a drawbridge on a moat

They never had enough courage, but one day they found it

They packed their gear with flashlights and snacks

As this castle was immensely massive

They said "it's time to discover what's inside"

Their only hope was to ensure that they live

They scaled the gate one by one

Carefully throwing over their backpacks

As they entered the grand entrance

They heard creeks, and moans, and the old floor had cracks

They yelled "who's in here?"

Then became silent awaiting a reply

Then just as they were ready to continue

They heard a woman cry

Continued…➡

Their face expressions stunned

As they looked at each other

Then a vision appeared

This was once someone's mother

She looked creepy and old

As their fear dissipated

Then she started to speak

As their breaths were all bated

She said don't be afraid

Of things you don't understand

Be courteous and kind

To your next fellow man

Then she disappeared

And they all went outside

As they carried her words

For the rest of their lives

The Ghost Inside Me

The ghost inside me, he is reaching for my hand

As I scribble words that I don't know, and I don't understand

Trust me I can't control it, he sometimes comes at night

And sometimes in the day, when the timing is not right

But I have to obey, there's nothing I can do

I just write the words he says to me until he is through

I sometimes read them back and get a shiver down my spine

I wonder where they come from and why he makes them rhyme

To be honest it's kind of cool how he occupies a small space in my soul

And not knowing when he'll visit is mysteriously unknown

At times I feel that he's a master by putting magic in my hand

Sometimes I feel confused, and I don't really understand

He says "it's time to go now and write this down"

My unfinished words will be the talk of the town

We've got great things to do just me and you

As he signed it. Sincerely, the ghost inside of you

R.I.P. 12/03/1965 – 2/12/2003

Chicky

He was tough and respected

He had that in spades

And everyone in the projects

Wanted to be in his parade

Everyone always asked

"What's Chicky doing today?"

Because they wanted to go along

In his imaginary band they wanted to play

He'd sleep outside for weeks

Just to see his favorite band

And when his friends needed tickets

He always had them in his hands

And the parties got so wild

People passed out in the woods

And when the kegs were beat

A little hungover, but man it was good

I was proud to call him my brother

"Chick" you finally made it in my book

I feel his presence shining down

As I take another look

What is it?

They say it is until it's not no more

If that is true, then what is it?

Is it the things that you love to do?

Or is it the things that you're trying to quit?

Some people say "it is what it is"

Intangible while you're trying to grab it

A tight rope walker losing balance

If it was true, well now behold it

Some people search a lifetime trying to find it

Only to find out in the end it was right there all along

They sing with glee their one hit wonder

It's on repeat their lifelong song

It fills their heart, it fills their soul

Evaporates and then it's back

It makes them think it's permanent

It pulls the rug across shellac

It really is a great big world

If that is true then what is it?

It's a masterful puzzle that puzzles the mind

As we search for the answer to find what is it

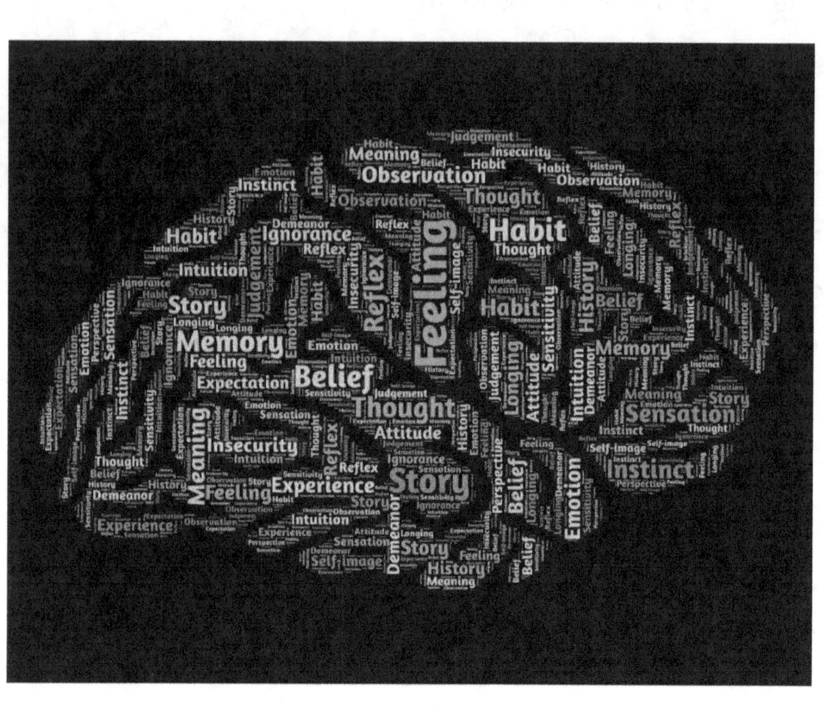

I Know Some Things

I know I wake up every day and try to be a better man

I know when people are in need I try to help out when I can

I know when someone is in pain my empathy begins

I know I'm not too good at losing but I can't always win

And even though I know some things

I know that I don't know everything … like

Why countries go to war when it's over stupid things

Why things can't stay just like they are without the golden ring

Why we feed other countries before we feed our own

Why we're spending so much money on nonsense while the homeless need a home

Why cancer isn't cured yet we've researched it many years

Why children get neglected and have to shed so many tears

Why pets can't find a home, and why they are being sold

Why can't we stay young forever, and why must we grow old

But I know …

We can be young at heart and take care of ourselves

Pay attention to what's important and never put it on a shelf

We can give someone a helping hand anytime that we can

And if there's something you don't understand, just try to understand

Lightning in a Bottle

Don't you think when your favorite band recorded your favorite song

They must have known that they captured lightning in a bottle

Even twenty years later when you crank it up to ten

It comes at you full throttle

The magic in the studio

How everything just fell in place

And when they heard the finished product

Can you imagine the looks upon their face

It's a once in a lifetime

Supernatural high

And when it hit the record stores

They just knew that it would fly

Everyone driving by them

They heard it blasting from their cars

It was like traveling through the universe

And they caught a falling star

I guess they rode the wave for as long as they could

Living life to the fullest, living at full throttle

But man do I wish I could have been a fly on that wall

On the day that they captured that lightning in a bottle

Catch a Falling Star

As I walked up the mountain

I caught a falling star

You wondered where I went

But it was everything you are

It was bright and radiant

As I held it in my hands

Of all the places it could have fell

And this is where it lands?

I was walking up the mountain

To get lost and find myself

The glow is getting much too bright

And I found something else

I heard your voice say "go back down"

But that was not my plan

As I contemplated what you said

While I held it in my hand

I closed my eyes and made a wish

And threw it way up high

Now it's right back where it belongs

Right beside you in the sky

False Confession

As he cried in disbelief
Stumbling around the chalk outline
All the CSI's were taking pictures
To construct an exact timeline

They brought him to the station
For a routine questioning
Then they slammed the door and got louder
With their hands rudely gesturing

They starved him for two days
As he begged them to find the killer
In his community he was well respected
Often referred to as a pillar

The detectives were relentless
And they finally broke his will
As they turned on the video camera
Weakly he whispered "I did kill"

Then they fed him, clothed, and showered
This respected innocent man
And they shipped him off to prison
In a padded unmarked van

Continued..➡

As twenty years went by

Just like the blink of an eye

Another man on his deathbed

Is making a confession as he cries

And in his final breath

He says he killed that woman back then

And the detectives and the prosecutors

Wrongly locked up an innocent man

When the man in jail heard this

He had a heart attack and died

And his ghost came back and haunted them

For the rest of their miserable lives

I Was There

The son made fun of his father

Just like he didn't care

Then he said "I'm fourteen years old now"

And the dad said "I know I was there"

The son looked confused

"Seven pounds, twelve ounces man I was scared"

You were the biggest baby I've ever had

I know cause I was there

One of my favorite pictures of you was your 1st birthday

There was cake on your face and everywhere

You were innocent and nothing but smiles

I took that picture cause I was there

You grew and wanted to try Cub Scouts

So I drove you here and there

You realized it wasn't for you

But still I was there

One day you ended up in Yale

One of the worst nights of my life and you had me very scared

They fixed you up and you came home

And once again I was there

Continued..➡

The son looked at the father

And said "dad I really do care"

The father smiled and walked away

As he said "son, I'll always be there"

The Paradox

The paradox it mocks its' soul

For it's not sure which way to go

A tug of war the flag not moving

It just stays put and not its choosing

Not knowing sometimes can be good

It introduces "what if I could?"

Be so bold, and be so loud

And dare to stand out in a crowd

I'd see the faces smiling at me

I'd be proud, and humble, and happy as can be

But if the flag starts moving in the wrong direction

I'd be in the back of the crowd in the nosebleed section

It teeters and totters and totters on teets

And its' teeth can be rotted from eating the sweets

If I had the decision just all mine to make

I promise you this, I would not forsake

I'd be clear and precise like I'm making a speech

With my words as my word as I further my reach

I'd be winning awards with my pats on my back

While I wish my momma well as I step on the cracks

Continued... ➡

You see the paradox it shifts and moves

And sometimes makes you lose your groove

So hold on tight and don't lose grip

There's one life to live and this is it!

The Wall

You went to the war

Could not give any more

As your comrades saw you fall

They put your name on a wall

Then your friend got shot down

He was always around

Another good one got the call

They put his name on the wall

And the medic tried real hard

But he lost all his cards

Another one took a fall

They put his name too on the wall

When the chopper came down

And the boots hit the ground

One by one they did fall

They put their names on the wall

And now everyone visits

Says a prayer and stands tall

For the bravery of the men

With their names on that wall

Alone

You asked me if I'd die for you

And I didn't know what to say

You looked upset and walked away

And then it finally hit me, just a minute too late

Without you there would be no sun

Without you there would be no moon

No picking flowers just because

No, I will see you soon

No colors in the rainbow

Just bland as bland can be

And who ever found the pot of gold

I assure you it wasn't me

The years would pass, and I'd ask around

Wondering if you've been seen

I got the news just like a dagger

And I knew the answer like awakening from a dream

I said "yes! I would die for you"

As I knelt before your stone

If you feel it, you must say it

Or you may end up all alone

The Bomb

Why would you build a weapon

That you never intend to use

Some evil dictator will come along

And he will light the fuse

As it sits there dormant

It's a silent killing machine

And with one push of the button

It can melt away your dreams

No more homes, and no more cars

No more possessions, and no more time

To have the things you've always wished for

Just one last breath, and one last rhyme

Just because you're smart enough to build it

Doesn't mean you should

They say money is the root of all evil

As it flies through the air they'll wish they could

Go back to the beginning

And throw away their plans

That they jotted down on paper

The most destructive weapon known to man

Continued... ➡

Now there's no way to press pause

And there's no way to go back

Poisonous gasses fill the air

And all the sky has turned to black

And just before the bomb hit the news said:

Put your heads between your legs and kiss your ass goodbye

And maybe in a million years

We can give it one more try

Heroes

Is it the thrill of the rush

Or the rush of the thrill

Hanging on to the edge

Without taking a spill

Running into the fire

Instead of running away

Then you're saving a life

As you're saving the day

Some people are just built different

And there's no way to explain it

Their circuitry is rewired

And their brain has retrained it

And their heart is something special

Like a rare anomaly

As they live life in color

They are brave, wild and free

They react and don't think

And don't think and react

Never once contemplating

That they won't be coming back

Continued...➡

Not looking for praise

Or awards on the wall

It's engrained in their DNA

They're not dropping the ball

Let's hope you don't need them

But if you do, they'll be there

Just a day in the life of a hero

It's the burden they bare

Worlds Collide

You got lost somewhere along the way

Caught between where worlds collide

Strapped on my helmet and fully tethered

But there's too many wormholes for you to hide

Humanity will carry on

But man, it was fun when you were around

As we listened to Smokey

With the tears of a clown

There's only so many days in a year

And so many years in a life

And this galaxy is way too big

So surrender thee under thy perjury of strife

I'm ready to be free

So when I say when, unhook my tether

The further I drift, the colder it gets

But I'm too numb to feel the weather

As I float away and drift too far

I just may pass you where you are

If you give it away and don't fight when it's taken

You'll be left with regret and remorse the forsaken

Memories

All the memories I have about you

When we met you said you were Haitian

You acted so crazy and wild

Like you were from an ancient civilization

The cupie dolls hair was cute

But yours was wilder and better

It was one hundred and twenty degrees

In the middle of July, you were wearing a sweater

Sweat running down your face

And you did not have a care

With the tropical winds blowing

All you kept asking is "How is my hair?"

We heard some music on the beach

You said it sounded like a steel drum

As I turned to see where it was coming from

When I looked back you started to run

As you danced around the fire

Just like you were back at home

Then you pulled me closer to you

And said promise to don't leave me alone

Continued…➡

The days went on forever

But the nights went by too fast

Before we knew it the summer was over

And like a dream I knew it couldn't last

Then you disappeared from my sight

And poof you were gone

But those memories will last forever

And in my heart you will carry on

Rain Falling

I feel the rain falling
It's just at my feet
I was heading out for the day
To get something to eat

As I turned to go back inside
It suddenly struck me
We've been having a drought
And I shouldn't decide so hastily

So I went back outside
Put my hands in the air
Felt the rain on my face
Without having a care

As I journeyed on my way
To get something to eat
I appreciated the rain
Falling down at my feet

And I felt all my sorrows
Wash away from the past
And in that instance I realized
I was happy at last

Sins of My Father

It's time to break the chain

I can't take it no more

No more screaming and yelling

And slamming of doors

You've been a bad little boy

Now I'm getting the belt

In the corner you go

Knees are bruised as I knelt

Now on to your mother

Time for kicking her ass

Now get up right now

And start cutting the grass

And I want to see lines

Just like a baseball diamond

As he rips apart your room

Looking for something he lost, but can't find it

I said when I get older

I'm gonna break the chain

He said good luck with that

You must be living a dream

Continued…➡

The years flew by fast

And I kept my promise

To him it felt like a threat

Being brutally honest

Now my children will never

Experience anything like my past

It's a beautiful world

Free at last, free at last

Star Traveler

I woke up to moonlight
And star light lit her eyes
As she dreamed in melancholy
An adventurous surprise

She said I've been there before
As she pointed towards north
And the bed started spinning
As she rocked back and forth

Then a glow made of moonbeams
Materialized over our head
As it lifted us up
Far away from the bed

Weightless and wonderful
Are two words that came to mind
As we traveled between the stars
A fantastical voyage, what a glorious find

She said "see that blue marble"
That was us back on earth
Until now would you have believed
It was not my origin of birth?

Continued...➡

We are choking her slowly

Finding it hard just to breathe

And this is the reason

That we had to leave

Mother earth she is shouting

Saying "stop this right now!"

As her screams fall on deaf ears

As we wonder just how

Could the greed of a nation

Extinct a completely whole planet

As we are no more

Now it's too late to ban it

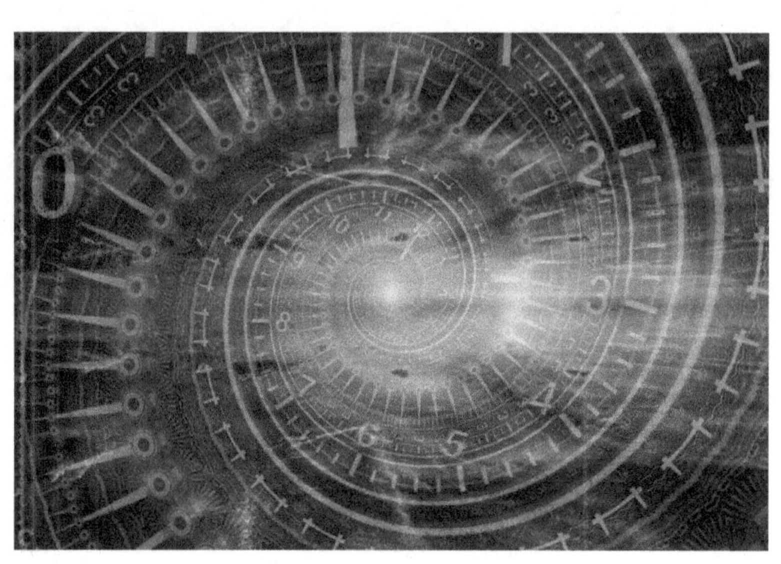

5 Minutes

What if you had 5 minutes
To go back in your past and change things
Would you squander it quick?
Or would you consider changing what your future could be

It's a hard decision
On what things to change
And the order of importance
And how the thereafter would be rearranged

But what a magnificent gift
To be given this chance
Would you get out of your seat
And ask her to dance?

Or would you go further back
To when you were young
And make a different choice
By holding your tongue

Because words do hold weight
Some too heavy to bear
Some you can't take back
And some will leave you with despair

Continued...➡

But you are the lucky one

You have 5 minutes to go back

As you contemplate what to do

Your sight turns to black

After careful consideration

You decided you won't change a thing

Because things happen for a reason

And what may come it will bring

But you will make better choices

From this moment on

As you give the gift back

With the wave of a wand

Finnish
Armenian
Continental Portuguese
Tahitian
Cambodian
Icelandic
Albanian
Cantonese
Tongan
Fijian
Spanish
Japanese
Polish
Frasi-Persian
Malagasy
Estonian
Mongolian
Serbian
Danish
Korean
Indonesian
French
Samoan
Afrikaans
Navajo
Hungarian
German
Italian
Ilonggo/Hillgaynon
Tagalog
Greek
Haitian Creole
ESL
Ukrainian
Russian
Hmong
Aymara
Mandarin
Cebuano
Brazillian Potuguese
Maori-New Zealand
Lithuanian
Norwegian
Latvian
Chinese
Roratonagan
Croation
Thai
Welsh
Romanian
Dutch
Guarani
Arabic
Bulgarian
Czech
Cakchiquel

Accents

People that have accents

Don't think they do

Until someone speaks differently

That's when they say, "Who knew?"

Some syllables are drawn out

Like "It's time to paak the caar"

As they try to reel it in

They don't always get too faar

Some will call you bloke

Sounding royally in the process

As they brag about the queen

She is the queen of no nonsense

Other accents you hear

Are cheerful boiling over

As they wear green for good luck

While picking a four-leafed clover

The next one you might hear

Is spicy and it's fun

Sometimes it takes a long time

There's so much rolling of the tongue

Continued... ➡

There are many more accents

For you to discover

Just open up your ears

And be a language lover

Irreplaceable Friend

Everything fixed can be broken

And everything broken can be fixed

Just put the ingredients in a bowl

And give it a mix

If the recipe comes out right

You'll have a beautiful disaster

It seems everyone is looking for

Their divine ever after

But don't look too deep

And don't look too far

What you think is just yours

Can't be kept in a jar

When it's ready to go free

You must let it fly

And some moisture may form

From the ducts of your eyes

And what's viewed as a heartbreak

Will soon start to mend

When by chance you should meet

An irreplaceable friend

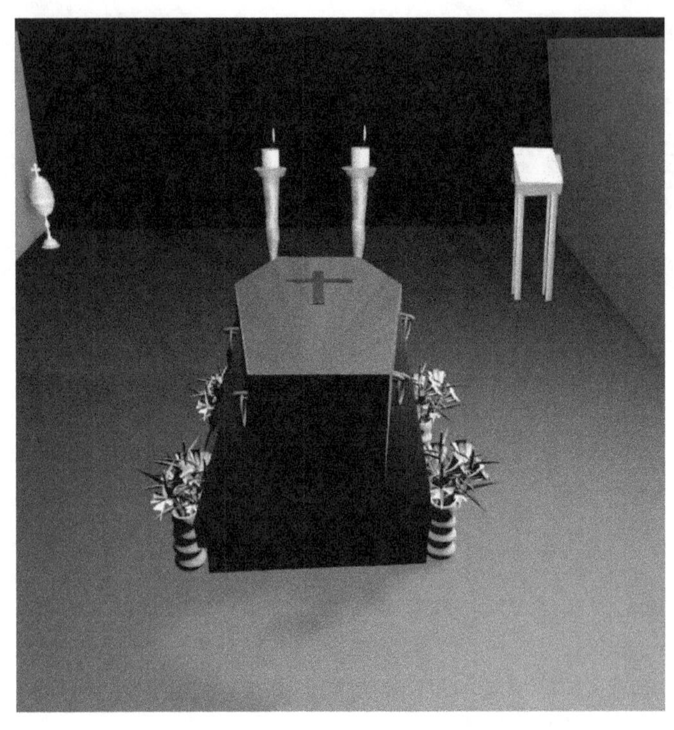

Immaculate Force

This is the tale of the wolf, the gator and the bear

One was cunning, one bite force, and one had no fear

And each one they will eat you

If you stumble, without care

The wolf he howls when creatures bring fright

Out in the full moon in the darkest of nights

But don't be fooled with the orange eyed stares

Just keep your composure and please do beware

The gator can chomp down just like a vice

With immaculate force not just once but yes twice

Once again keep your distance and stick to your wits

We are strong, move along, as this can be it

The bear can be burly with claws like a knife

And a hug can be deadly squeezing air out your life

And you don't want to hear those intangible sounds

Of the straps and the gears lowering you into the ground

Horns of a bull

It eats, and it eats

But never seems to get full

And digs deep down inside of you

Like the horns of a bull

You say, "God make it stop!"

But it seems to push on

Like a train in the night

Lights the way until dawn

But it doesn't seem fair

When it happens to you

It just keeps ravaging on

What a shame, all these schools

Where's the Einstein of medicine?

The guru resident within

While it's creeping and crawling

Living under your skin

One day we will sleep

And awaken revealed

Lays his hand on your head

And says, "my child you are healed"

Fly to the Angels

It's time for you to rest your eyes

And just give up the fight

You've been struggling with this for far too long

A million, thousand nights

The rope has frayed and wound up as

A fishing line sized string

It's okay now, you can let go

Watch the water ripple as you toss the ring

Like it never was

Or will it ever be?

We live our lives

With unusual things

We call them possessions

But do they really possess us?

When we finally lose them

We just cry and fuss

And kick and scream

And make a scene

It feels just like

We've lost our dreams

Continued...

So, hush my love don't say a word

Too many are wasted and have already been spoken

And the fragility of life has taken its toll

The impenetrable force field was bound to be broken

Go fly to the angels

Dissipate and go fly free

The lesson was learned

What shall be … shall be

Fruitful Life

I woke up this morning

To tangerine skies

As I looked to my left

It was the apple of my eye

With curves like a peach

And parts like a pear

And those great watermelons

Had me gasping for air

She had channeled Cleopatra

And along came the asp

Holding on to her cantaloupes

As I continued to gasp

She said life's not a cher-i-bowlies

Reaching down for the fig

As the leaf flew away

And so did her wig

Well sometimes life gives you lemons

And sometimes you get limes

So have a drink and be merry

And enjoy your fruitful life

Don't Judge a Book by the Cover

You might read this book and say

"This guy must be mad"

You might read another poem and say

"This one makes me sad

When you opened up the cover

You didn't know what to expect

But now you're in too deep

You turn the page to see what's next

This one makes you soar

Without ever leaving your seat

His words are wild and wonderous

Now you're sinking in your teeth

One interruption while reading

Will make you lose your freaking mind

A treasure chest all filled with gold

The plot gets thicker, a jewel you find

One that you carry with you

All throughout your life

Now this one taught you lessons

They live down deep inside

Continued... ➡

All because your instincts ruled

And you didn't judge the book by the cover

Enlightenment and emotions abound

Just follow your heart and not this, that and the other

Hold on to the Roses

A concubine, a twist in time

Just write it down, the words will rhyme

Just let it flow, then you will know

That this is how, the poem goes

Don't intervein, don't be too mean

Afterall, we all have dreams

Sometimes they're small, sometimes you fall

Make sure you're ready, for your curtain call

Yes it will come, don't be undone

When they call your name, just run, run, run

But do not trip, and do not stumble

Remember to, always stay humble

Cause that big ole ego, will swallow you up

And it will runneth over, and "it" is your cup

 You got this man!, you got this lady!

Since you were born, this was your baby

So nurture it, and do not quit

Perseverance is life, and life is this

The path was written, before you were born

 Hold on to the roses, but watch out for the thorns

Grief

What's right or wrong?

Or wrong or right?

I take this grief

Into the night

And dig a hole

To bury it

It sinks in claws

And it won't quit

I push it down

Into the hole

It climbs back out

And won't let go

I get enraged

And swear at it

Now go now grief!

You piece of shit!

It then retreats

And quits the fight

I finally rest

My tired eyes

Continued...➡

Sometimes you have to

Push on through

Demolish the walls

And start a new

Cause the baggage gets heavy

And a burden to carry

Take a breath of fresh air

The unknown can be scary

Extortion

She made up lies

She made him cry

I know you don't believe this

Because they say that men never cry

He gave up his fortune

To keep his fame

He played along

As he played her game

The wife never found out

Because there was nothing to tell

He shielded his children from the tabloids

She put him through hell

All because of a made up lie

And a man's integrity

To be not too proud to cry

Not too proud to fall

This happens more than you may think

When the scum of the earth make that call

MICHEL NOSTRADAMUS.
Médecin,
Né à S.ᵗ Remy, en Provence, le 14 Décemb. 1503.
Mort le 2 juillet 1566.

No Nostradamus

He said you want to see me set fire to the rain

Watch me do it

He said there's many miracles in this brain

Yes I've been through it

I've walked with giants many abound

Whose heads were in the clouds

Sadly, some are no longer around

But they wore their badges proud

Some have called me Nostradamus

But that is just not me

Many visions have come before my eyes

That others just could not see

That does not make me a prophet

A wizard, or even a saint

I've dealt with what life has thrown at me

A god is what I ain't

Follow your path and your dreams will grow

So unimaginable and flourish

Keep the faith that feeds your soul

And keeps your body nourished

When it's time, it's time

If you believe the story of your life

Was written before you were born

All the journeys of your life

You will face and carry on

Some things will knock you down

But you will get back up

If your glass always stays half full

Well at least you have a cup

There will be many achievements

There will also be many tears

For many different reasons

That will last throughout the years

But if you stay steadfast in your beliefs

And wake every day to carry on

You'll live with no regrets

To face another dawn

And when the time finally comes

When nothing seems to rhyme

He'll gently put his hand on your shoulder

And whisper, when it's time "it's time"

I am Free

While climbing up the mountain

To search for the holy grail

I saw a pile of ashes

As my visions grew, they began to tell their tales

Of monuments that stood so tall

And majestic bridges to connect you to them

And of leaders with integrity

And a free world that we lived in

With calloused hands and sweat on brows

And every stake they hammered in

And every war they had to fight

They knew somehow they had to win

They named the states one by one

And built a mighty nation

"Houston are you coming in?"

They exclaimed over television stations

And here we sit with a pile of ashes

Of all that used to be

As I continue on with my climb

Thanking God that I am free

The Most Toys

Once around the world

Although once was not enough

All that's important in this life

Cannot be totaled into stuff

If you end up with the most toys

Do you really win?

Outside they see you smiling

But inside's a crooked grin

Collecting all your jars of hearts

And cars they stretch for miles

Tennis courts, arcades, and pools

Is that really what makes you smile?

Would you be willing to lose it all?

And accept a different love

Do you attribute it all to a higher power?

Looking down from up above

Well if not my friend, then try this once

Sleeping out on the street

With nothing in your pockets but lint

And not a bite of food to eat

Continued...➡

Do you really think?

That you can survive

Or will you gain a new perspective

And thank God that you're still alive

It's time to reevaluate

Now is the time for switching gears

And choose a new trajectory

To be the one who cares

Tennessee Whiskey

She listens to "Tennessee Whiskey"

Every time she gets depressed

She likes to play it on vinyl

She says that's the way it sounds the best

On the porch she'll watch the stars

And imagines faces in the moon

Like it's winking right back at her

As the music makes her swoon

She then points at Mr. Firefly

Trying to time out when he lights

Like a beacon blinking for lost souls

Saying prayers for one more night

Then she makes her way slowly towards the pool

And says "I'll think I'll take a dip"

As her sultry eyes stare through my soul

Simultaneously biting her lip

When the morning comes the vinyl's still spinning

Like a broken record with unheard of delight

And there's no more sign of depression

Not one ounce of it in sight

Continued… ➡

I guess that Tennessee Whiskey

Must have really cheered her up

As we dance into the daylight

Pouring good spirits in our cups

Rainbow

What's the bow without the rain?

What's the pain without the tears?

Even when the crowds are gone

It's been there for all these years

It retreats into the background

Displaying skies so bright and blue

But when the world is feeling sad

It reappears with its' magnificent hues

Bringing hope to those who've lost it

And dreamers dream inspired by the sight

For all who see, they'll never forget it

No discussion anymore of what's wrong and what's right

Remembering the brilliant colors

And what it took to make them

Have galvanized their reasons being

No more shall the rain ever break them

I Lost Me

Some people say that I lost me

But I can't see just what they see

I waved my arms, I'm still here! I'm still here!

But you looked right at me like you didn't care

I stood there in bewilderment

As the mirror showed me my reflection

I swear to god I'm right here!

As thoughts flood my mind with recollections

Of innocence and skipping school

And bumper riding in the snow

And singing Christmas Carols

And getting slices of pizza with the dough

Back to a simpler time

Where I was who I was

No influencing or convoluting

My skin fit tight just like a glove

But things fill your mind

Then move on to your body

And twist your molecules

And start to make things shoddy

Continued...➡

I think it's time to go back now

To the real me

So no one ever says again

That I somehow lost me

Starlight Glory

I went around the bend

And then back to the beginning

Losers lose the call

Starlight glory for the winning

Nestled in bosoms

Nature beckons the call

Jester's joking a clown

With his red nose and all

And the symbols are crashing

And the band's in a tizzy

Symphony of destruction

Swaying 'round makes me dizzy

Will it trade? If a trade is

From a dollar to a dime

Turns it back like a clock

Waves his hand it is time

Rides the Ferris wheel

In the clouds his head is high

Looking for the little people

As it all passes him by

Continued…

And then goes to a swap meet

Gets an autographed Babe Ruth

Puts his tokens in the bus

Man, I'm telling you the truth

Leopards losing his spots

As he pukes in the sink

Squints his eyes from the pain

While he's getting the ink

No more happy endings

Watch me skimboard on a whale

This is getting out of hand

It is time to end this tale

Honesty

It sometimes hurts

It's sometimes raw

For some a hard decision

To make that call

It is truth

Sometimes hard to be

But let it out

And it will set you free

Some keep it inside

Until it's too late

Some never speak it at all

And create their own fate

Some just don't know

Or where to start

So they hold it inside

Until it tears them apart

But when it finally is told

They feel so relieved

What we're talking about

It is honesty

A Christmas Tale

You knew I couldn't let you go

Without an awesome Christmas Tale

The bells they started ringing out

As the trumpets began to wail!

He's here! He's here!

The children shouted out with glee!

The big red suit and the big white beard

Putting presents under the tree

He turned around and they ducked and hid

As they should have been fast asleep

Then he turned, and left, and flew away

In their hearts there was magic to keep

As their parents yelled "I hope you kids are in bed"

They slid under the covers and closed their eyes

So they could awaken Christmas morning

To collect their wonderful surprise

Free pictures provided by pixabay

Cover Design: selfpubbookcovers.com/ Viergacht

Chicky picture by Theresa Hayes

I would like to thank everyone for your support.

In the literary world without you there is no me.

Billy J. Barnum

If you like this book, please check out my other books. Thank you!

Please visit www.talesfromthebaron.com

ABOUT THE AUTHOR

Billy J. Barnum has released two poetry books to date and is still referred to as "the simple man's poet". His words, verses, and prose are easy to understand and do not require a dictionary to comprehend.

His poetry is meant to elicit a reaction or a feeling and may also start a conversation in book clubs or classrooms when reading his works.

It is rumored that if he has nothing to write then the pages will sit blank for as long as it takes. Once the words, ideas and visions start flowing it is hard to turn off the spigot. By the last poem in his last book, we didn't know if there would be any more poems or any more books but, I guess "The Ghost Inside Him" just wouldn't let him rest. So come one, come all in true Barnum fashion and get the new Tales from the Baron and immerse yourself in wonderment and delight.

(Picture taken by Orion Storm Barnum)

Dream Big!